Essential Words

D0490490

SCIENCE

NEW LEAF

THE INTERNATIONAL SCHO
OF THE HAGUE
Primary School
Jan Willem Frisolaan 4
New Leaf Education 2517 JS 's-Gravenhage
P. O. Box 16230
Baltimore, Maryland 21210

New Leaf Education has a special offer on new products
for people on our mailing list.
Go to www.newleafeducation.com to learn more.

Design and Cover Illustration:
Ophelia M. Chambliss
Oliver Bliss Design

Printed in the United States of America

10 9 8 7 6 5 4 3 2 1

NEW LEAF

Contents

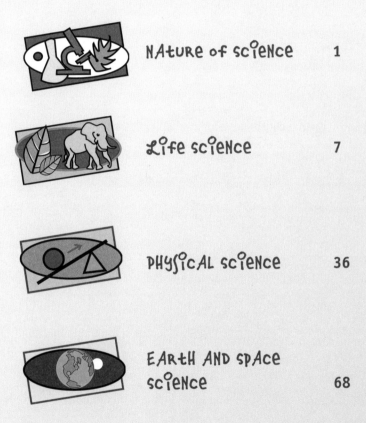

Essential Words

welcome to tHe

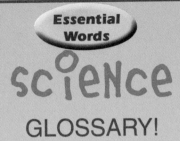

Essential Words
scieNce
GLOSSARY!

ABOUT THE BOOK

Here is a glossary to help you learn the Essential Words in Science that you will need to be successful in school. These Essential Words will also help you succeed on state tests. There are more than 200 Science words in the book! They are listed in alphabetical order under four main topics.

Here is a sample word with its features:

Easy-to-read definitions

Examples in context

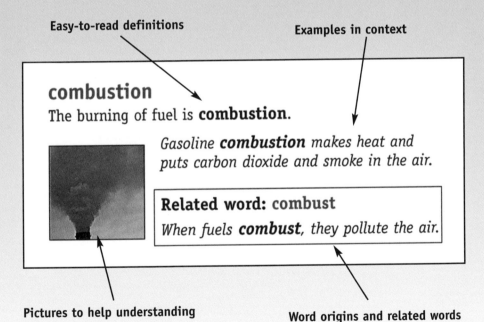

combustion
The burning of fuel is **combustion**.

*Gasoline **combustion** makes heat and puts carbon dioxide and smoke in the air.*

Related word: combust
*When fuels **combust**, they pollute the air.*

Pictures to help understanding

Word origins and related words

We hope that you will find this book easy to use and enjoyable. Tell us what you think. We would love to hear from you!
www.newleafeducation.com

Nature of Science

constant

When scientists do an experiment, they often compare two groups. Everything about the two groups should be the same, except for what the scientists are studying. A **constant** is something that is the same for both groups.

*Some scientists did an experiment with two groups of chicks. They gave Food A to one group and Food B to the other group. Each group had the same number of chicks, the same temperature, and the same amount of space. That means that the number of chicks was a **constant**. Temperature and space were also **constants**.*

Word Roots and Origins

The ending of *constant* comes from a Latin word meaning "stand." To be constant is to stand still and not change. A constant does not change from one group to another.

data

Data are pieces of information. Scientists collect **data** about what they observe. **Data** are often in the form of measurements.

*The masses of the chicks on different days were **data** from the chick experiment.*

	Food Type	Average Mass Day 7 (g)	Average Mass Day 14 (g)	Average Mass Day 21 (g)
Group A	A	150	175	200
Group B	B	150	200	250

evidence

Evidence is information that shows something. It is a sign that something is true.

The chicks in Group B gained mass faster than the chicks in Group A. This is **evidence** *that Food B helps chicks grow faster than Food A does.*

hypothesis

A **hypothesis** is an educated guess about what will happen. A scientist has a **hypothesis** before he or she begins an experiment.

The **hypothesis** *for the chick experiment was that Food A would help chicks grow faster than Food B would. However, it was the chicks eating Food B that grew faster. This showed that the* **hypothesis** *was wrong.*

Related word: hypothesize

When you decide or say what your hypothesis is, you **hypothesize**.

The scientists **hypothesized** *that Food A would help chicks grow faster. In their next experiment, they will probably* **hypothesize** *that Food B will make chicks grow faster.*

magnitude

The size of a measurement is its **magnitude**. A measurement has a number and a unit, and it may have a direction. The number and unit make up the **magnitude**. The **magnitude** does not tell direction.

*If a chick's mass is 200 grams, the number of the measurement is 200 and the unit is grams. The **magnitude** of the mass is 200 grams.*

*You go forward and backward on a swing. You go just as fast backward as you do forward. The **magnitude** of your velocity forward is the same as the **magnitude** of your velocity backward. Only the direction of your velocity changes.*

Word Roots and Origins

Magna means "great" or "large." The magnitude of something is how large it is.

---

model

A **model** can be a picture, a graph, or a solid figure. It can even be a thought or a mathematical equation. A **model** stands for something and makes it easier to understand. It **models** something that is being studied.

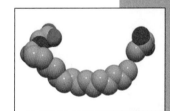

*This large **model** of a molecule shows its shape and its different parts.*

*You can use a graph to **model** the results of an experiment.*

*In the modern **model** of the Solar System, the planets revolve around the Sun.*

observation

You make an **observation** when you notice something. Scientists make **observations** when they study things or do experiments.

When two groups of chicks were given different foods, one group grew faster than the other group. This was one **observation** *made during the chick experiment.*

Word Roots and Origins

Ob means "in the way," and *serve* comes from the Latin word that means "to keep." If you keep in the way of something, you can watch what happens to it.

Related word: observe

Scientists need to **observe** *what happens in an experiment and write down what they notice.*

technology

Technology is science put to work. Engineers and inventors use science to make things that people use. **Technology** is the process of making those things.

*Engineers use **technology** to make TVs, cars, and medicines.*

*Physics is the science that deals with matter and energy and how they interact. The **technology** of making cars is based on the science of physics.*

*Satellite dishes for TVs are **technology** based on what scientists know about waves.*

theory

A scientific **theory** is an explanation of something that most scientists agree with. It is not just a guess. Scientists test **theories** to see if they are true and to learn more. Sometimes they learn things that make them change a **theory**.

*Before the germ **theory** of disease, people did not wash their hands very often.*

*The cell **theory** states that all living things are made up of one or more cells.*

Related word: theorize

*Scientists **theorize** that stars begin as huge clouds of gas and dust.*

variable

In an experiment, the **variable** is what the scientists vary, or make different, so they can study its effect.

*Some scientists did an experiment with two groups of chicks. Everything about the two groups was the same, except the food. One group ate Food A, and the other group ate Food B. Food was the **variable** so that the scientists could study the effects of the two different foods.*

Related word: vary

*When you **vary** something, you make it different.*

*Every week, my school activities **vary**. On Monday, I have gym, but on Tuesday, I have art.*

abiotic

Something is **abiotic** if it is not living and has never been living.

*Rocks, air, and water are **abiotic**. Things made by people are also **abiotic**.*

adaptation

An **adaptation** is a trait that helps a plant or animal survive.

*Every elephant has a long trunk that allows it to collect food from high in trees. An elephant can also curl its trunk around a clump of grass and pull it up by its roots. The long trunk of an elephant is an **adaptation**. It allows the elephant to reach food in many places.*

> **Related word: adapt**
>
> *Animal species **adapt** over time. Plant species also **adapt** to the world around them.*

antibiotic

An **antibiotic** is a medicine that kills bacteria. **Antibiotics** are used to help cure diseases that are caused by bacteria.

*The doctor can give you **antibiotics** for your strep throat, but not for your cold.*

> **Word Roots and Origins**
>
> *Anti* means "against," and *bio* means "living." Antibiotics are used against living germs.

bacteria

Bacteria are very small living things. They have only one cell and cannot be seen without a microscope.

*Some **bacteria** make you sick, but you need other **bacteria** to keep you healthy.*

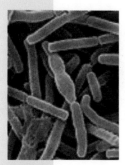

Word Roots and Origins

The word *bacteria* comes from the Greek word *bacterion*, which means "small stick." Under a microscope, some bacteria look like sticks.

Related word: bacterium

Bacterium is the singular form of *bacteria*. One **bacterium** can split and become two bacteria.

behavior

An animal acts and reacts to the world around it. How an animal acts and reacts is called its **behavior**. An animal is born with some **behaviors** and learns others.

*Building a web is a **behavior** of many spiders.*

Related word: behave

*People who study spiders want to know how they **behave**.*

Life science

biodiversity

The number of different kinds of living things in an area is called **biodiversity**. An area with many different types of plants and animals has much **biodiversity**.

*Rainforests have great **biodiversity**. There are 117 different kinds of trees in just one-half of a square mile of the Amazon rainforest.*

> **Word Roots and Origins**
>
> *Bio* means "living" and *diversity* means "differences" or "mix of different things."

biosphere

The **biosphere** is the part of the Earth where living things can stay alive. Most of the **biosphere** is near the surface of the Earth. However, some of the **biosphere** is underground, and some is high in the air.

*The ocean is the largest part of Earth's **biosphere**. Many different plants and animals live in the ocean **biosphere**.*

biotic

Anything that is living is **biotic**.

*Plants, animals, and people are **biotic** parts of the environment.*

camouflage

Camouflage is a color or pattern on an animal that lets it hide by blending into the background.

*A polar bear's white fur coat is perfect **camouflage** for its home on the ice and snow.*

carbon

Carbon is a chemical element that is found in all living things.

***Carbon** flows through the environment in a cycle. In the air, **carbon** is part of **carbon** dioxide. It flows into plants during photosynthesis, and the **carbon** becomes part of the plants. Animals that eat plants take **carbon** into their bodies, and it becomes part of them. Some of the **carbon**, as part of **carbon** dioxide, leaves the animals when they breathe. It goes back into the air, and the cycle begins again. This flow is a part of the **carbon** cycle.*

Life science

cell

A **cell** is the basic unit of life. All living things are made of one or more **cells**.

A single-celled organism is made of just one **cell**. *Multicellular organisms are made of many kinds of* **cells**. *For example, people have muscle* **cells**, *skin* **cells**, *nerve* **cells**, *fat* **cells**, *and more.*

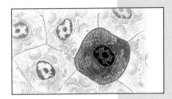

Word Roots and Origins

Another meaning of *cell* is "small room." Many living cells have a rectangle shape, like a tiny room.

chlorophyll

Chlorophyll is a green substance inside green plants. It helps plants change sunlight, water, and carbon dioxide into food.

Most plants are green because of the **chlorophyll** *in them, especially in their leaves. It is important in photosynthesis.*

Word Roots and Origins

Chloro means "green," and *phyll* means "leaf."

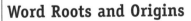

chromosome

Chromosomes are found inside living cells. They contain genes, which control what living things look like and what they do.

*There are 46 **chromosomes** in a human cell.*

classification

Classification is the grouping of things that are alike. **Classification** of animals puts animals that are alike in the same group.

*Tuna and goldfish both have scales and live in water. The **classification** of animals puts tuna, goldfish, and other animals like them in the same group.*

> **Related words: classified, classify, class**
>
> *Animals that have feathers and lay eggs are **classified** as birds.*
>
> *You can **classify** plants by the shapes of their flowers and leaves.*
>
> *Mammals make up a **class** of animals.*

combustion

The burning of fuel is **combustion**.

*Gasoline **combustion** makes heat and puts carbon dioxide and smoke in the air.*

> **Related word: combust**
>
> *When fuels **combust**, they pollute the air.*

community

A **community** is made up of all the living things that share an area.

*The forest **community** includes trees, birds, and mammals. They live in the same place and affect each other.*

conserve

To **conserve** something is to use it wisely and to not waste it.

*We should **conserve** our clean water so it lasts a long time.*

*Riding the bus instead of driving a car **conserves** energy.*

Word Roots and Origins

Conserve is from a word meaning "keep" or "guard." When we conserve our resources, we keep some of them for later or for others to use.

Related word: conservation

*Energy **conservation** leaves fuel for others. It also reduces air pollution.*

consumer

A living thing that eats plants or animals is a **consumer**.

*A deer is a **consumer** that eats plants.*

*A cougar is a **consumer** that eats deer.*

decomposer

A **decomposer** breaks down dead plants and animals and the wastes of living things.

*Dead leaves are broken down to carbon and other chemicals by **decomposers** in the soil. Many insects and worms are **decomposers**.*

Word Roots and Origins

Compose means "put together," as a musician will compose music by putting together notes. *De* means "undo" or "do the opposite." To decompose is to do the opposite of putting together, that is, to take something apart or break it down.

DNA

DNA is a molecule that is found inside cells. It looks like two long threads twisted together. **DNA** contains genes, which carry the information that cells need to live.

*Identical twins have exactly the same **DNA**.*

Word Roots and Origins

DNA stands for "d̲eoxyribon̲ucleic a̲cid."

ecosystem

An **ecosystem** is made up of all the living and nonliving things in an environment. All of these things interact in an **ecosystem**.

*The Zhelvata River **ecosystem** in Russia includes fish, birds, mammals, water, trees, soil, and air.*

embryo

A living thing in the first stage of development is an **embryo**. Only organisms with more than one cell go through this stage.

*An animal is an **embryo** right after fertilization of the egg cell.*

endangered species

An **endangered species** is a species that is in danger of becoming extinct.

*The tiger is an **endangered species.** There are very few tigers left in the wild.*

*It is illegal to harm a member of an **endangered species.***

Related word: endanger

*Cutting down the forest will **endanger** many types of plants and animals. They will be put in danger.*

energy

Energy is the capacity to do work.

*Plants use the **energy** from sunlight to do the work of making sugar.*

*We use electrical **energy** to make our computers and machines work.*

*We use the **energy** stored in fossil fuels to heat our homes.*

Life science

environment

The **environment** of a living thing is everything around it. Air, water, soil, plants, and animals are parts of the **environment**. It also includes things like temperature, rainfall, and light.

*When we protect the **environment**, we protect ourselves.*

*Earthworms live in soil, in a dark and moist **environment**.*

> **Related word: environmental**
>
> ***Environmental*** *factors such as light and moisture affect all living things.*

evolution

Evolution is the change of a species over time. A species is a group of individuals that can mate with each other and produce offspring.

*The **evolution** of the horse has taken millions of years.*

Hyracotherium
(50 mya)

Mesohippus
(25 mya)

Hipparion
(8 mya)

Pliohippus
(4 mya)

Equus
(recent)

> **Related words: evolve, evolved**
>
> *Species can **evolve** as their environments change.*
>
> *Many scientists think that birds **evolved** from dinosaurs.*

Life science

extinct

A species of living thing that has died out is **extinct**. When a species becomes **extinct**, there are no more members of that species left alive on Earth.

*Dinosaurs have been **extinct** for 65 million years.*

*The wild parakeets of North America became **extinct** about 100 years ago.*

Related word: extinction

*Scientists think that the **extinction** of the dinosaurs could have been caused by a giant rock that smashed into Earth from space.*

*Today scientists and others are trying to prevent the **extinction** of pandas.*

---

fertilization

Sexual **fertilization** is the joining of an egg cell and a sperm cell.

Fertilization is the first step in sexual reproduction.

*Some insects can reproduce without **fertilization**.*

Related word: fertilize

When birds reproduce, the first step is for a sperm cell to **fertilize** an egg cell.

Life science

food chain

A **food chain** is the path energy takes as it flows from one living thing to another in food. A **food chain** shows what animals eat and what they are eaten by.

*In this **food chain**, seals eat fish and are eaten by polar bears.*

food web

A **food web** is many different food chains in an ecosystem connected. They form a **food web** because they affect each other.

*This **food web** shows that large fish are eaten by both sharks and humans.*

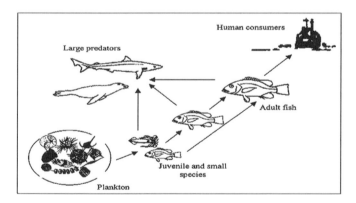

fungi

There are many kinds of **fungi**, which all get their food from living or dead organisms or their wastes. The kingdom of **fungi** includes molds, mushrooms, and yeasts.

*Baker's yeast is one of the useful **fungi**.*

Related word: fungus

Fungi is the plural form of ***fungus***.

*The white mushroom sold at the grocery store is a tasty type of **fungus**.*

*Some types of **fungus**, like the "toadstool," will make you sick.*

---

gene

A **gene** is a small part of a DNA molecule that carries instructions for one trait. For example, we have **genes** for eye color.

*Children get half of their **genes** from their mothers and half of their **genes** from their fathers.*

Word Roots and Origins

The word *gene* comes from the Greek word *genos*, which means "birth."

At birth we have all the genes we will ever have.

Related words: genetic, genetics

*Eye color is **genetic**. It is passed to us from our parents.*

*The study of genes and heredity is called **genetics**.*

Life science

habitat

A **habitat** is the place where something lives or the type of environment it usually lives in.

*Bat **habitats** include dark, cool, moist caves.*

*The desert **habitat** of the kangaroo rat is hot and dry, with few plants.*

> **Related word: inhabit**
>
> *Many squirrels **inhabit** trees.*
>
> *Our basement is **inhabited** by crickets.*

heredity

Heredity is the passing of traits from parents to offspring. **Heredity** affects what we look like, how we act, and how healthy we are.

*His blue eyes are due to **heredity**. His mother has blue eyes too.*

> **Related words: hereditary, inherit**
>
> *Curly hair is **hereditary**.*
>
> *If your father has curly hair, you may **inherit** curly hair.*

life cycle

The **life cycle** is the circle of events from birth to parenthood. It begins with one generation and begins again with the next generation.

*The **life cycle** of a butterfly is not simple. A butterfly begins life as an egg, then becomes a larva, then a pupa, and then an adult butterfly. Adult males and females can mate, and the females can lay eggs. Then the **life cycle** starts again with each new egg.*

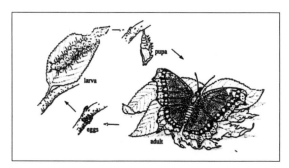

metamorphosis

Metamorphosis is the change in shape that happens to some animals as they grow into adults.

*A butterfly goes through **metamorphosis** as it changes from an egg to a larva to a pupa to an adult.*

Word Roots and Origins

The word *metamorphosis* comes from two roots. *Meta* means "change," and *morph* means "form."

Related word: metamorphose

*Tadpoles **metamorphose** into frogs. They lose their tails as their form changes.*

microorganism

Any living thing that is too small to see without a microscope is a **microorganism**.

Bacteria are too small to see with the naked eye. They are ***microorganisms***.

Word Roots and Origins

Micro means "very small," and *organism* means "a living thing."

Related word: microbe

Another word for *microorganism* is **microbe**.

A ***microbe*** *is a very small living thing.*

---

natural selection

If a living thing has traits that help it survive in its environment, it is likely to live longer than others and have more offspring. It passes those helpful traits to its offspring, and they pass them to their offspring. Eventually, the helpful traits become common. This is the process of **natural selection**.

Because of ***natural selection***, *very few tigers are born without orange and black stripes. These stripes help tigers blend in with tall grass and trees. When tigers blend in, they are better hunters.*

nonrenewable resource

Any part of the environment that we use and that we cannot replace is a **nonrenewable resource**.

*Coal, oil, and natural gas are **nonrenewable resources** because we cannot make more of them.*

Related words: renewable resource

A **renewable resource** is the opposite of a nonrenewable resource. We can replace it.

*Wood is a **renewable resource**. We can plant more trees when we use them.*

---

nucleus

The nucleus is the part of the cell that controls what the cell does. The **nucleus** contains DNA.

*Without a **nucleus**, a cell cannot make new cells.*

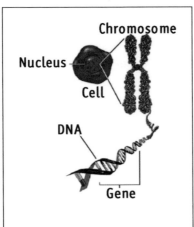

nutrient

A **nutrient** is a chemical substance that the body needs in order to live.

*Carbohydrates, proteins, fats, water, vitamins, and minerals are the six types of **nutrients** we need.*

Related word: nutrition

Nutrition is the process of getting all the nutrients you need.

*For good **nutrition**, it is a good idea to take a vitamin tablet.*

---

offspring

Offspring are the "children" of people, animals, or plants. **Offspring** share traits with their parents.

*The **offspring** of dogs are called puppies.*

*The **offspring** of most plants start life as seeds.*

organ

An **organ** is a part of the body that performs a certain job. The heart, lungs, stomach, and even skin are all examples of **organs** in the human body.

*The heart is an **organ** that pumps blood around the body.*

*In most fish, gills are the **organs** that bring in oxygen.*

Word Roots and Origins

The word *organ* comes from Greek words meaning "tool" and "work."

---

organ system

A group of organs that work together is an **organ system**.

*The digestive system is the **organ system** that includes the esophagus, stomach, and intestines.*

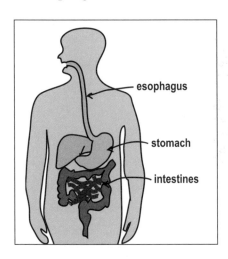

esophagus

stomach

intestines

organism

An **organism** is any living thing.

Plants and animals are examples of multicellular **organisms**. They are made up of many cells that do different jobs.

Bacteria are examples of single-celled **organisms**. In bacteria, all the jobs are done by the same cell.

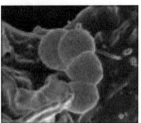

*Sore throats can be caused by a single-celled **organism** called* Streptococcus.

oxygen

Oxygen is a chemical substance that most living things need. It is not a nutrient, but we cannot live without it. When we breathe, we push out carbon dioxide and pull in **oxygen**.

*Trees are important because they make a lot of the **oxygen** we breathe.*

photosynthesis

Plants make food by a process called **photosynthesis**. They use the energy from sunlight to turn water and carbon dioxide into food and oxygen.

*Without **photosynthesis**, there would be much less oxygen in the air.*

Word Roots and Origins

The word *photosynthesis* has two roots. *Photo* means "light," and *synthesis* means "put together." In photosynthesis, plants use the energy from light to put together carbon dioxide and water to make sugar.

Related word: photosynthesize

*Plants need light in order to **photosynthesize**.*

---

pollination

Pollination is the transfer of pollen from the male part of a seed plant to the female part of a seed plant. **Pollination** allows plants to make seeds.

*Some plants need insects to help in **pollination**.*

Related words: pollen, pollinate

Pollen is the powdery substance that develops into plant sperm cells.

*When bees carry **pollen** from flower to flower, they help **pollinate** them.*

*Many people are allergic to **pollen**. It makes them sneeze.*

pollute

We **pollute** the environment when we make air, water, or soil unclean with our waste.

*Smoke and gases from factories **pollute** the air.*

*We **pollute** the water with chemicals, heat, and trash.*

*When gasoline leaks from underground tanks, it **pollutes** the soil.*

Related words: pollution, pollutant

Pollution is the act of making the environment unclean with waste products.

***Pollution** by cars can make the air unsafe to breathe.*

We call the waste products **pollutants**.

*Hybrid cars make smaller amounts of **pollutants**.*

---

population

A **population** is a group of the same kind of plant or animal living together in the same place.

*Antarctica is home to a large **population** of emperor penguins.*

Related words: populate, overpopulate

Populate means "to live in" and also "to provide with members."

*Emperor penguins **populate** Antarctica.*

*An **overpopulated** area does not have enough food, water, or space for everyone.*

predator

A **predator** is an animal that hunts and eats other animals.

*Lions are important **predators** in Africa.*

> **Related word: predation**
> **Predation** is the act of hunting to eat.
> ***Predation** by owls is killing off the mouse population.*

prey

To hunt and eat an animal is to **prey** upon the animal.

*Falcons **prey** upon birds.*

Also, the animal that is hunted and eaten is called the **prey**.

*The falcon caught its **prey**.*

producer

A **producer** is a living thing that makes its own food. It uses energy to put together chemical substances to make sugar or other food.

*Plants are **producers.** They use the energy from light to put together carbon dioxide and water to make sugar.*

Life science

renewable resource

Any part of the environment that we need and that we can replace is a **renewable resource**.

*Meat and vegetables are **renewable resources**. Farmers raise more of them when we eat them.*

Related words: nonrenewable resource

A **nonrenewable resource** is the opposite of a renewable resource. We cannot replace it.

*Fossil fuels are **nonrenewable resources** because we cannot make more of them.*

---

reproduction

Reproduction is the process that makes others of the same kind. **Reproduction** can be sexual or asexual. Sexual **reproduction** makes offspring that get half of their genes from each parent. Asexual **reproduction** makes copies of one parent.

*Sexual **reproduction** in cats makes kittens. Kittens do not all look like their mothers.*

*In asexual **reproduction** of bacteria, one splits and makes two exactly alike.*

Related word: reproduce

*When dogs **reproduce**, they make puppies.*

Words Roots and Origins

Re means "do again," and *produce* means "make." So reproduce means to make again or make another.

smog

When sunlight acts on smoke and gases from cars, it makes a type of air pollution called **smog**.

*During the summer the **smog** in Los Angeles can be so bad that you can see, smell, and taste the air.*

Word Roots and Origins

Smog is a combination of the words *smoke* and *fog*.

---

species

A **species** is a group of living things that can mate and have offspring. ***Species*** is both singular and plural.

*All dogs belong to the same **species**.*

*Cardinals and robins are different **species** of birds.*

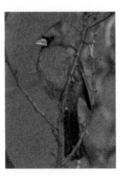

sunlight

The energy that we get from the Sun is **sunlight**. Plants need **sunlight** to make food. And we need plants to make food and oxygen for us. **Sunlight** energy in the form of heat evaporates water and forms clouds. Without heat from **sunlight**, there would be no rain for the plants.

*Without **sunlight**, we would not be able to live on Earth.*

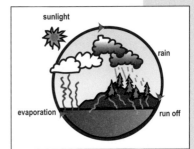

tissue

A **tissue** is a group of similar cells that work together to do the same job in the body.

*In our bodies there are muscle **tissue**, fat **tissue**, and nerve **tissue**.*

*Cells make up **tissues**, the **tissues** make up organs, the organs make up organ systems, and the organ systems make up organisms.*

trait

A genetic **trait** is a characteristic that is passed from parent to offspring. **Traits** include eye color, hair curliness, and height. The instructions for each **trait** are carried on the DNA in each living cell.

*Red hair is a **trait** that parents can pass on to their children.*

*Striped leaves is a **trait** that is sometimes seen in plants.*

vaccine

A **vaccine** is a substance that helps the body fight off germs that cause diseases.

*Getting a flu **vaccine** can help to keep you from getting the flu.*

Word Roots and Origins

Vaccine comes from the Latin word *vacca*, which means "cow." The first vaccine was made from a virus that made cows sick. It made people slightly sick, but it also helped them fight off a much worse disease called smallpox. So people used the cowpox germs as a vaccine against smallpox.

Related word: vaccinate

You **vaccinate** people when you give them a vaccine.

*It is important to **vaccinate** your dogs and cats against rabies.*

virus

A **virus** is a small particle that invades a cell and causes illnesses. A **virus** is not a living thing, but it can make copies of itself when it gets into a cell.

*Most colds are caused by **viruses**.*

Word Roots and Origins

In Latin the word *virus* means "venom" or "poison." A poison kills or hurts the living thing it enters. A flu virus can kill people, and a cold virus can hurt people by making them sick.

Related word: viral

*The flu is a **viral** disease. It is caused by a virus.*

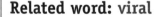

Life science

waste materials

In general, **waste** is what is left over when living things use something. There are many types of **waste materials**. The parts of food that we don't eat are **waste**. The feces that come from animals after they digest their food are **waste**. The chemicals left over when factories make things are **waste.**

Waste materials from food contain a lot of carbon and nitrogen. The wastes are broken down by decomposers in the soil. Then the nitrogen can be used again in plants. When the carbon wastes burn, they give off carbon dioxide, which also can be used by plants.

Waste disposal becomes a problem when we make more wastes than nature can recycle.

accelerate

When something speeds up or slows down, it **accelerates**.

*Our car can **accelerate** from 0 to 60 miles per hour in 10 seconds.*

*When you drop a ball, it **accelerates** until it hits the ground.*

Word Roots and Origins

The word *accelerate* comes from the Latin word *celer*, which means "fast."

Related word: acceleration

*Our car has good **acceleration**.*

*On Earth the **acceleration** due to gravity is about 10 meters per second per second. This means that every second that something falls, it speeds up by 10 meters per second.*

---

alloy

An **alloy** is a mixture of elements that has metallic properties. Most **alloys** are mixtures of metals.

*A gold ring is made from a gold **alloy**. It is made by mixing gold with copper, zinc, nickel, or silver.*

Word Roots and Origins

The word *alloy* comes from the Latin word *alligare*, which means "bind."

Related word: alloyed

Copper is often **alloyed** with gold to make jewelry.

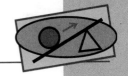

atom

An **atom** is the smallest piece of an element. **Atoms** are the building blocks of matter.

*Water is made of hydrogen **atoms** and oxygen **atoms**.*

Word Roots and Origins

The word *atom* comes from a Greek word that means "uncuttable." If an atom of an element is cut into smaller pieces, it is no longer that element.

Related word: atomic

*An **atomic** bomb explodes when the nuclei of atoms split in two.*

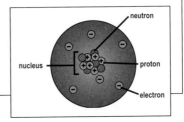

---

boil

When a liquid **boils**, it turns into a gas.

*Water **boils** at a temperature of 100°C.*

Word Roots and Origins

The word *boil* comes from the Latin word *bullire*, which means "bubble." Water bubbles when it boils.

Related words: boiling point

The temperature at which a liquid boils is its **boiling point.**

*The **boiling point** of water is 100°C.*

carbon

Carbon is a chemical element. It is present in all living things. A **carbon** atom is made up of six protons, six neutrons, and six electrons.

Carbon atoms bond to each other and to other types of atoms.

Word Roots and Origins

The word *carbon* comes from the Latin word *carbo*, which means "ember." Wood is mostly carbon. Burning wood has glowing embers.

Related words: carbon dioxide

Carbon dioxide is a gas in the air. Plants take in **carbon dioxide** to make food. Animals breathe out **carbon dioxide.**

---

chemical

A **chemical** is made up of one or more atoms. A **chemical** is an element or a compound. Many **chemicals** are natural, but many are made by people.

*Water is a **chemical** made up of two hydrogen atoms and one oxygen atom.*

*The **chemicals** in the air include oxygen, carbon dioxide, and water.*

chemical bond

The force that holds two atoms together is called a **chemical bond**.

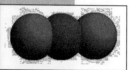

*This is a model of a carbon dioxide molecule. One carbon atom and two oxygen atoms are held together by **chemical bonds**.*

PHYSICAL SCIENCE

Related words: bond, bonded

To **bond** two things is to hold them together.

*Glue can **bond** two pieces of paper together.*

*Water is made of oxygen and hydrogen atoms that are **bonded** together.*

---

chemical change

In a **chemical change**, old bonds between atoms break and new bonds form. Two or more substances change into a new substance.

*When wood burns, the wood combines with oxygen and makes charcoal. Charcoal is the result of the **chemical change**.*

Related words: chemical reaction, react, chemical property

A chemical change happens during a **chemical reaction**.

*When wood burns, wood combines with oxygen in a **chemical reaction**.*

*When wood burns, wood and oxygen **react**.*

The ability of a substance to change into a new substance is called a **chemical property**.

*Being able to burn is a **chemical property** of wood.*

*Being able to rust is a **chemical property** of iron.*

circuit, electric

An **electric circuit** is a complete path that lets electric charges move. The electric charges move because there is a power source pushing them. The electric charges that move in a wire are electrons.

The light in a room comes on when you make an **electric circuit** *by flipping the light switch.*

In the diagram of an **electric circuit***, the power source is a battery.*

combustion

Combustion is burning. It happens when a substance combines with oxygen and produces heat and light.

In a car, **combustion** *happens inside the engine. The gas burns inside the engine and produces heat.*

Related words: combust, combustible

Gasoline **combusts** *easily. It is dangerous to have flames near gasoline because it is* **combustible***.*

Word Roots and Origins

Combust comes from the Latin word comburere, which means "burn."

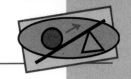

compound

A substance that is made of two or more types of atoms that are bonded together is a **compound**.

*Salt is a **compound**. It is made of sodium and chlorine atoms that are bonded to each other.*

*Water is a **compound**. It is made of hydrogen and oxygen atoms that are bonded to each other. Water is also a molecule because it has covalent bonds.*

condense

When a gas turns into a liquid, it **condenses**.

*When water is a gas, it is called water vapor. When water vapor in clouds **condenses**, it makes rain.*

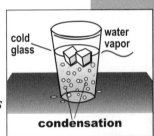

Related word: condensation

*There is **condensation** on my glass. There are tiny drops of water all over it.*

conductor, electrical

An **electrical conductor** is a substance that electrons can move through easily.

*Electricity flows through a **conductor**.*

*Metals are very good **electrical conductors**. That is why they are used to make electrical wires.*

Related word: conduct

*Copper **conducts** electricity very well. Electrons flow through copper very easily.*

conductor, heat

A **heat conductor** is a substance that heat can move through easily.

*Metals are very good **heat conductors**. If a cool metal object touches a hot object, it will get hot very quickly.*

Related words: conduct, conduction

*Air does not **conduct** heat very well. Water **conducts** heat better than air does.*

*When a metal frying pan is placed on a hot burner of a stove, the pan is heated by **conduction**.*

---

convection

The movement of heat by the flow of a hot substance is called **convection**.

*Some rooms are heated by **convection**. Hot air flows away from a heater to colder parts of the room.*

crest, wave

The wave **crest** is the highest point of the wave.

*When a tsunami reaches the beach, the **crest** of the wave can be ten meters high.*

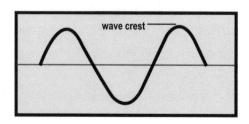

wave crest

crystal

A **crystal** is a solid whose atoms are bonded in a pattern that repeats. The repeated pattern makes regular geometric shapes. Some **crystals** are too small to see. Others are large.

Quartz **crystals** *have six sides. Calcite* **crystals** *also have six sides, but they are not shaped like quartz.*

Related words: crystalline, crystallize

Granite is **crystalline** *rock. It is made of crystals.*

Salt **crystallizes** *from salt water. The crystals form after the water evaporates.*

---

current, electric

An **electric current** is a flow of electrons from one place to another.

For a lamp to shine, there must be an **electric current** *in its wires. Electrons must flow through the wires.*

Word Roots and Origins

The word *current* comes from the Latin word *currere,* which means "run."

Electrons run through the wire when there is an electric current.

density

Density is a measure of how tightly matter is packed. For two objects with the same mass, the one that takes up less space has the greater **density**.

*You can find the **density** of a rock by dividing its mass by its volume.*

*Rock has a much higher **density** than plastic foam does.*

> **Related words: dense, denser**
>
> *Even though the rock was small, it was very heavy because it was so **dense**.*
>
> *If two objects are the same size, the one that is **denser** weighs more.*

electricity

Electricity is the movement of electrons. **Electricity** is a form of energy. In a wire the energy is in the form of an electric current.

*TVs and computers need **electricity** in order to work.*

electromagnetic radiation

Electromagnetic radiation is a form of energy that travels through space as a wave.

*Radio and TV waves, microwaves, light, and X rays are examples of **electromagnetic radiation**.*

> **Related words: electromagnetic spectrum**
>
> The range of all the forms of electromagnetic radiation is called the **electromagnetic spectrum**.
>
> *The **electromagnetic spectrum** begins with radio waves and ends with gamma rays. Visible light waves are a very small part of the **electromagnetic spectrum**.*

PHYSICAL SCIENCE

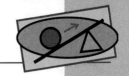

electron

An **electron** is a particle in an atom. **Electrons** are found moving very quickly outside the nucleus of an atom. An **electron** has almost no mass, but it has a negative charge. When **electrons** move from atom to atom, they create an electric current.

A carbon atom has six ***electrons***.

element

An **element** is a substance that is made of only one kind of atom. There are 92 different **elements** that occur naturally on Earth.

Carbon is an ***element***. *Carbon is made up of only carbon atoms.*

Hydrogen and oxygen are both ***elements***. *Water is not an* ***element***. *It is made up of the* ***elements*** *hydrogen and oxygen.*

energy

Energy is anything that can make things happen. There is **energy** in living things and in nonliving things. There are many different forms of **energy**.

Heat and light are forms of ***energy***.

Food contains chemical ***energy***.

evaporate

When a liquid turns into a gas, it **evaporates.**

When the Sun comes out, all of the puddles will ***evaporate***.

> **Related word: evaporation**
> ***Evaporation*** *caused the surface of the lake to drop.*

force

A **force** is a push or a pull. A force can make something move or change direction. There are many different kinds of **force**. These include gravitational **force**, magnetic **force,** and electrical **force**.

*The **force** of gravity pulls objects toward each other.*

freeze

When a liquid turns into a solid, it **freezes**.

*When the temperature of liquid water drops to 0°C, it begins to **freeze**.*

Related words: frozen, freezing point

*The water has **frozen**. It is now ice.*

The **freezing point** of a liquid is the temperature at which it freezes.

*The **freezing point** of water is 0°C.*

---

frequency

The **frequency** of a wave is the measurement of the number of crests that pass in one second. The **frequency** of a pendulum is the number of times it swings back and forth in a second.

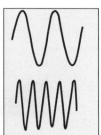

*In the picture, the wave on top has a lower **frequency** than the wave on the bottom.*

> **Related word: pitch**
>
> The frequency of a sound wave is also called its **pitch**.
>
> *The **pitch** of a sound tells you how high or low the sound is.*
>
> *The sound of a whistle has a high **pitch**. Thunder has a low **pitch.***

friction

Friction is a force that slows down an object or stops it when it rubs against another object.

*A ball will stop rolling across the grass because of **friction**.*

*You can slide on ice because there is not much **friction** between the ice and your shoes.*

> **Word Roots and Origins**
>
> The word *friction* comes from the Latin word *fricare*, which means "rub."

gas

A **gas** is a substance with no shape or size. The molecules in a **gas** are very far apart. They move apart to fill up the available space.

*We filled the balloon with helium **gas**.*

*Air is made up of many **gases**.*

> **Word Roots and Origins**
>
> The word *gas* comes from the Greek word *khaos*, which means "empty space." There is a lot of empty space between molecules in a gas.
>
> **Related word: gaseous**
>
> *When water is in its **gaseous** form, it is called water vapor.*

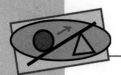

gravity

Gravity is the force that pulls two objects toward each other.

*Earth's **gravity** keeps people from flying off into space.*

Related word: gravitational

Gravitational *force keeps the planets in orbit around the Sun.*

---

half-life

Some atoms decay, or break down, to form new atoms. The **half-life** of a substance is the time it takes for half of its atoms to decay.

*Uranium-238 has a **half-life** of about 4.5 billion years. In 4.5 billion years, there will be only half as many uranium-238 atoms as there are now.*

*Carbon-14 has a **half-life** of just 5,730 years. There were twice as many carbon-14 atoms 5,730 years ago as there are today.*

heat

Heat is a form of energy that moves from a warm object to a cold object.

*We burn wood and oil to turn their energy into **heat** energy to warm our homes.*

***Heat** from inside the Earth heats the houses in Iceland.*

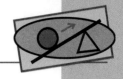

hydrogen

Hydrogen is the smallest element known. It is made up of one proton and one electron.

Hydrogen bonds with oxygen to make water.

*The **hydrogen** gas in the Sun burns and sends energy to Earth and the other planets in our solar system.*

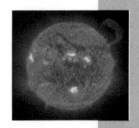

insulator, electric

A substance that stops electrons from moving from one place to another is called an **electric insulator**. Rubber, glass, and plastic are **electric insulators**.

*Plastic is used as an **insulator** on the outside of electric wires. It stops the electricity from moving into your body.*

> **Related word: insulation**
>
> *Electric wires are covered with **insulation** to prevent electric shock.*

insulator, heat

A substance that stops heat from moving from one place to another is called a **heat insulator**. Fiberglass, wool, and plastic foam are **heat insulators**.

*Plastic foam is used as an **insulator** in walls. It stops heat from leaving the building.*

> **Related word: insulation**
>
> *Many attics contain fiberglass **insulation**. In winter it stops heat from leaving through the ceiling. In summer it stops heat from coming in.*

ion

An **ion** is an atom that has gained or lost one or more electrons.

*A sodium atom has 11 protons and 11 electrons. But a sodium **ion** has 11 protons and only 10 electrons.*

lens

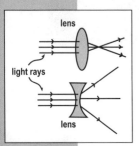

A **lens** is a piece of glass or plastic that focuses or spreads out light rays. **Lenses** are used to make things easier to see.

*The **lenses** in a microscope make objects look much bigger than they really are.*

*People who wear glasses may wear contact **lenses** instead.*

Word Roots and Origins

The word *lens* is Latin for "lentil." Some lenses are shaped like lentils.

light

The energy that we can see is called light or visible **light**. We need **light** in order to see.

*People can't see in the dark, but cats can see when there is very little **light**.*

*White light is made up of all the colors of **light**.*

*You can use a mnemonic, ROY G BIV, to remember the colors of the visible **light** spectrum.*

Word Roots and Origins

The word *light* comes from the Greek word *leukos*, which means "white."

liquid

A **liquid** is a substance that has a shape that changes but a volume that does not change.

*Coffee, tea, and milk are all **liquids.***

*When you pour a liter of **liquid** from a bottle into a pan, the shape of the **liquid** changes. But there is still a liter of **liquid**.*

Word Roots and Origins

The word *liquid* comes from the Latin word *lixa*, which means "water." Liquids flow like water.

magnet

An object that can attract iron is a **magnet**.

Horseshoe **magnets** and bar **magnets** are often used in science classes.

*A **magnet** on the refrigerator will hold up a note or a picture.*

*A compass used for finding direction has a floating **magnet** that points north.*

Related words: magnetic, magnetism, magnetize

*The Earth has a north **magnetic** pole and a south **magnetic** pole.*

*A substance that can attract iron has the property of **magnetism**.*

*You can **magnetize** an iron needle by passing a **magnet** across it.*

mass

Mass is the amount of matter in something. **Mass** is measured on a balance.

*The more **mass** an object has, the harder it is for you to move it.*

matter

Matter is anything that has mass and takes up space. You and every object around you are made of **matter**.

*Soil, air, milk, books, clothing, and ink are all made of different types of **matter**. **Matter** is made up of atoms. Air and ink are made up of different combinations of atoms.*

melt

When something **melts**, it turns from a solid into a liquid.

*When ice cream **melts**, it drips down the cone.*

*When the weather is warm, snow **melts** and water collects in lakes and streams.*

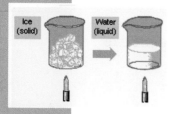

Related words: melting point

The **melting point** of a solid is the temperature at which it begins to melt.

*The **melting point** of water (ice) is 0°C.*

metal

A **metal** is a substance that is shiny, conducts heat and electricity, and bends without cracking.

*Steel is a **metal** made out of iron and carbon. Iron is also a **metal**.*

Related word: metallic

Something **metallic** is like a metal.

*Some clothes are so shiny that they look **metallic**.*

*Graphite is not a metal, but it has the **metallic** property of conducting electricity.*

---

mixture

A **mixture** is a combination of two or more pure substances. Those substances do not bond. The **mixture** has properties of the pure substances.

*Salt water is a **mixture** of salt and water. It tastes salty and looks just like pure water.*

molecule

A **molecule** is a compound held together by covalent bonds.

*A water **molecule** is made up of two hydrogen atoms and one oxygen atom.*

*Ethane is usually a gas. An ethane **molecule** is made up of two carbon atoms and six hydrogen atoms.*

*Glucose is a solid. A glucose **molecule** is made up of six carbon atoms, twelve hydrogen atoms, and six oxygen atoms.*

Related word: molecular

*Water is made up of molecules, so it is a **molecular** substance.*

*This model of ethane is a **molecular** model.*

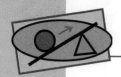

neutron

A **neutron** is a particle that is found inside the nucleus of an atom. It has no charge and about the same mass as a proton.

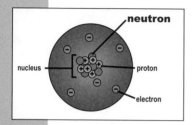

*A carbon atom has six **neutrons**.*

nitrogen

Nitrogen is a chemical element. A **nitrogen** atom is made up of seven neutrons, seven protons, and seven electrons.

*There is a lot of **nitrogen** in muscles.*

*About 78% of the Earth's atmosphere is **nitrogen** gas.*

nucleus

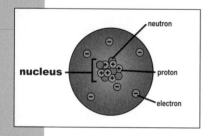

The center of an atom is called its **nucleus**. It is filled with protons and neutrons. It is surrounded by electrons.

*The **nucleus** of an atom contains nearly all the mass of the atom. The **nucleus** contains all of the atom's positive charge.*

Related words: nuclei, nuclear, nuclear reaction

Nuclei is the plural of *nucleus*.

*In one atom there is one **nucleus**. In two atoms there are two **nuclei**.*

Nuclear energy is energy that comes from the nucleus of an atom. A **nuclear** power plant uses it to make electricity.

A reaction that involves a change in the nucleus of an atom is a **nuclear reaction**.

*When the nucleus of a uranium atom is split, that **nuclear reaction** gives off energy.*

oxygen

Oxygen is a chemical element. An **oxygen** atom is made up of eight protons, eight neutrons, and eight electrons. Two **oxygen** atoms bonded to each other make up an **oxygen** molecule.

Oxygen is a gas that plants make and that people and animals must breathe in to stay alive.

*Air is about 21% **oxygen** gas.*

> **Related word: oxygenate**
>
> When you put **oxygen** into something, you **oxygenate** it.
>
> *We need to **oxygenate** the water in our fish tank so the fish can breathe.*

physical property

You can measure a **physical property** of a substance without changing it. Odor, color, and mass are **physical properties.**

*You can use **physical properties** to tell the difference between orange juice and milk.*

*Chemists can often tell what a substance is by measuring its **physical properties**.*

pole

Poles are the two regions of an object that have the strongest effects that are opposite each other.

*A bar magnet has a north **pole** and a south **pole**.*

*The Earth is a giant magnet. It has a north magnetic **pole** and a south magnetic **pole**.*

potential energy

Potential energy is energy that something has because of its position or shape.

*When a book is lifted, the book gains **potential energy**.*

*A stretched rubber band has more **potential energy** than a loose rubber band.*

power

Power is how fast work can be done. **Power** is work divided by time.

*When you move something, you do work on it. When you move it faster, you use more **power**.*

*If two trucks move bricks, the truck with more **power** can move more bricks in an hour.*

*It takes more **power** to lift 200 pounds in one second than in two seconds.*

Related word: powerful

*A 100 watt fan is twice as **powerful** as a 50 watt fan.*

pressure

Pressure is the amount of force that pushes against a certain area. **Pressure** is force divided by area.

*When you push harder on the door, you put more **pressure** on it.*

*Deep in the ocean, the water **pressure** is high because water pushes in from all directions.*

property

A **property** is a trait of a substance. Color and melting point are **properties**. How a substance behaves with other substances is also a **property**.

*The element gold has many important **properties**. It is bright yellow and very dense. It can be pounded into thin sheets. And it does not easily react with other elements.*

> **Related words: physical property, chemical property**
>
> ***Physical properties** include color and density.*
>
> *A **chemical property** is the ability to burn.*

proton

A **proton** is a particle that is found inside the nucleus of an atom. It has a positive charge and about the same mass as a neutron.

*All oxygen atoms have 8 **protons**. All gold atoms have 79 **protons**.*

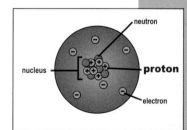

radiation

Energy in the form of waves or particles is **radiation**.

Radiation from the Sun gives us light and can tan or burn our skin.

Radiation also means the transfer of energy by waves.

*The **radiation** of heat from a space heater can warm up a room.*

> **Related words: radiant, radiate**
>
> *Stars are **radiant** bodies in the sky. They send out light waves.*
>
> *Space heaters give off **radiant** heat.*
>
> *Stars **radiate** energy in the form of light and heat.*

radioactivity

Energy given off by the nuclei of atoms is **radioactivity**.

*You can measure the **radioactivity** of uranium or radium.*

> **Related words: radioactive, radioactive decay, radiometric dating**
>
> An atom is **radioactive** if it gives off energy as particles or waves from its nucleus.
>
> *Radium is **radioactive**. Uranium is also **radioactive**.*
>
> **Radioactive decay** is the natural release of energy from the nuclei of atoms. It can be used to determine the ages of rocks. This is called **radiometric dating**.

reflect

To **reflect** is to throw something back. It also means to be thrown back.

*A mirror will **reflect** light. Light will **reflect** from a mirror.*

*A wall **reflects** sound. Sound is **reflected** by a wall.*

Related word: reflection

*When you look at yourself in a mirror, you see your own **reflection**.*

*You can see the **reflection** of a mountain in a lake below it.*

refract

The path of light will bend when it moves through one thing into another. When a light beam moves through air and into glass, it moves in a different direction. When the light **refracts**, it changes its path or bends.

*Light will **refract** when it goes from air into water.*

*Light is **refracted** by glass.*

Related word: refraction

*A rainbow is caused by the **refraction** of light when it moves from air into water droplets and back into the air.*

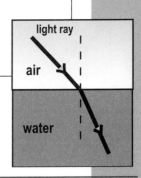

light ray

air

water

resistance

Resistance is the force that works against the flow of an electric current.

*Conductors have very little **resistance**. They let current flow freely.*

*Insulators have very high **resistance**. They can stop electric current.*

Related word: resistor

A **resistor** is put in an electric circuit to control the flow of the electric current.

---

semiconductor

A substance that has traits of both insulators and conductors is called a **semiconductor**.

*Silicon is a **semiconductor** used in computers and cell phones. It allows some current to flow. It controls the current so that there is not too much.*

Word Roots and Origins

Semi means "half." A semiconductor may let only half as much current get through as a conductor would.

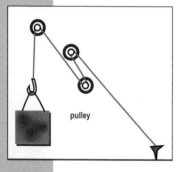

pulley

simple machine

A **simple machine** is one of six types of machines: inclined plane, lever, pulley, screw, wedge, and wheel and axle.

*All machines are made by combining more than one **simple machine**.*

PHYSICAL SCIENCE

solid

A **solid** is a substance with definite shape and volume.

*When water freezes, it becomes ice, which is a **solid**.*

When a substance is not a gas or a liquid and is not hollow, it is **solid**.

*An empty box is not **solid**, but a brick is.*

solubility

The **solubility** of a substance is the amount of it that can dissolve in something else. For example, sugar will dissolve in water. More sugar will dissolve when the water is hot. This means that heat increases the **solubility** of sugar in water.

***Solubility** usually tells you how much of a substance can dissolve in water at 25°C at sea level.*

Related words: dissolve, soluble, solute, solvent, solution

*Sugar **dissolves** when you put it in hot water and stir it. It seems to disappear, but you can taste that it is there.*

*Oil is not **soluble** in water. It does not seem to disappear.*

*Sugar is the **solute** in a sugar water solution.*

*Water is the **solvent** in a sugar water solution.*

*The sugar and water together make a **solution**.*

sound

Sound is a sensation, like touch or taste. **Sound** is also a set of vibrations that travel as waves through air and other substances. When the vibrations reach your ears, you hear them.

*When a guitar string vibrates, it makes a **sound**.*

*A **sound** wave can travel through a gas, liquid, or solid, but it cannot travel through outer space.*

speed

Speed is the rate at which something moves. **Speed** is distance divided by time.

*A fast car can travel at a high **speed**.*

*Turtles don't have much **speed**. They move slowly.*

Related word: velocity

Velocity is speed with direction.

*When you tell how fast and which way a car is moving, you tell the **velocity** of the car.*

state

The form that a substance is in is called its **state**. There are four **states** of matter: solid, liquid, gas, and plasma.

*When water evaporates, it changes **state**. It changes from a liquid to a gas.*

*When ice is heated, it goes from a solid **state** to a liquid **state**.*

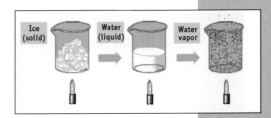

trough, wave

The wave **trough** is the lowest point of a wave. ***Trough*** rhymes with *off*.

*When the boat was in the **trough** of the large wave, the wave looked like a wall of water.*

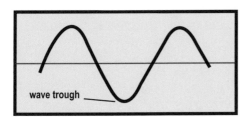

vaporization

The change of state from liquid to gas is called **vaporization**. A vapor is a gas.

*In **vaporization**, liquid water becomes water vapor.*

> **Related word: vaporize**
>
> *Water will **vaporize** faster when it is heated.*

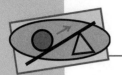
velocity

The speed of an object in a certain direction is its **velocity**.

*The **velocity** of the jet is north at 460 miles per hour.*

Related word: speed

Speed is velocity without direction.

*The **speed** of the jet is 460 miles per hour.*

---

vibration

The back-and-forth movement of an object is called **vibration**.

*The **vibration** of air in a trumpet produces music.*

*In an earthquake, **vibrations** travel through the ground.*

Related word: vibrate

*When you hit a drum, it **vibrates** and makes a sound.*

*An earthquake can make buildings **vibrate** so much that they fall down.*

viscosity

The **viscosity** of a substance is its resistance to flow. The higher the **viscosity**, the slower a fluid will flow.

*Thick motor oils have high **viscosity**.*

*A liquid with a high **viscosity** seems to stick to itself.*

Related word: viscous

*Honey is more **viscous** than water.*

---

wave

A **wave** is a disturbance in matter or space. The **wave** moves energy from one place to another.

*A rock thrown into water disturbs the water and makes **waves**.*

*At the ocean, large **waves** can push you over with their energy.*

*Light and sound travel as **waves**.*

wavelength

A **wavelength** is the distance from one wave crest to the next crest.

*The **wavelength** of an ocean wave is several meters.*

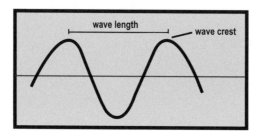

weight

Weight is a measure of the force of gravity. **Weight** tells how much something is being pulled toward the center of Earth. **Weight** increases as mass increases.

*If you eat too much, you might gain **weight**.*

*Elevators have **weight** limits. They cannot lift too many people.*

> **Related word: weigh**
>
> *I need to **weigh** these apples to be sure that I buy two pounds.*
>
> *This bag of apples **weighs** two pounds.*

work

When you push or pull an object and it moves in the direction you push or pull, you do **work** on the object. **Work** is force times displacement.

*You do a lot of **work** on a car when you push it up a hill.*

*You can get very tired without doing any **work** if the car does not move.*

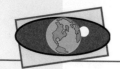
acid rain

Acid rain is unclean rain that can hurt plants, animals, and buildings.

Acid rain is damaging the buildings in Athens, Greece.

Word Roots and Origins

The word *acid* comes from the Latin word *acere,* which means "to be sour." Things that are acidic (like lemons) taste sour.

aquifer

A layer of rock or sand that holds water under the surface of Earth is called an **aquifer**.

*People who live in Florida get most of their water from the Floridan **aquifer**.*

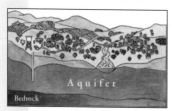

Word Roots and Origins

The word *aquifer* comes from the Latin word *aqua*, which means "water."

asteroid

An **asteroid** is a large rock in space. Most **asteroids** travel around the Sun between Mars and Jupiter.

*Ceres is the largest **asteroid**.*

asthenosphere

Earth's surface is broken into large pieces called plates. These plates are layers of rock that move over a layer below. That layer below is called the **asthenosphere**. The **asthenosphere** is one part of Earth's mantle.

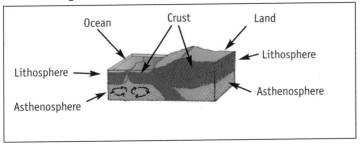

*Scientists think that the rocks in the **asthenosphere** are partly melted.*

Word Roots and Origins
Asthenes is the Greek word for "weak." The rocks in the asthenosphere are weak, so they can flow.

atmosphere

An **atmosphere** is a thin layer of gas that surrounds a planet.

*Earth's **atmosphere** protects us from the harmful rays of the Sun.*

Word Roots and Origins
Atmos is the Greek word for "vapor" or "gases." *Spheros* is the Latin word for "hollow ball." The atmosphere is a ball of gases that is hollow except that it contains the planet Earth.

axis

An **axis** is an imaginary line that runs through the center of a planet. A planet rotates about its **axis**.

*Earth's **axis** is tilted.*

biosphere

The **biosphere** is the part of the Earth where living things can stay alive. Most of the **biosphere** is near the surface of the Earth. However, some of the **biosphere** is underground, and some is high in the air.

*The ocean is the largest part of Earth's **biosphere.***

carbon cycle

Carbon is an element that is found in living things, rocks, and air. Atoms of **carbon** do not stay in the same place forever. They move. The same **carbon** atom can be part of the air, then part of a plant, then part of an animal, then part of a rock, and then part of the air again. This is called the **carbon cycle**.

*Scientists worry that burning too much coal puts the **carbon cycle** off balance.*

Related words: carbon dioxide

Carbon dioxide is an important gas in Earth's atmosphere. It is also important to the carbon cycle. It is made of carbon and oxygen. Plants use **carbon dioxide** to make food. Animals breathe **carbon dioxide** back out into the air.

EARth AND spAce scieNce

climate

The kind of weather an area has most of the time is its **climate**.

Parts of Brazil have a hot and rainy **climate**.

Related words: climatic, climatology, climatologist

Anything related to **climate** is **climatic**.

Scientists who work at the **Climatic** *Research Unit study the Earth's climate.*

These scientists study **climatology.**

They are **climatologists.**

---

combustion

Combustion is burning. It happens when a substance combines with oxygen and produces heat and light.

In a car, **combustion** *happens inside the engine. Gas burns inside the engine and produces heat.*

Word Roots and Origins

Combustion comes from the Latin word comburere, which means "burn."

Related words: combustible, combust

It is dangerous to have flames near gasoline because gasoline is **combustible**.

Gasoline **combusts** *easily. That is, it burns easily.*

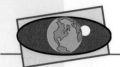
comet

A **comet** is a piece of ice, dust, and rock that orbits the Sun.

*The tail of a **comet** always points away from the Sun.*

condense

When a gas turns into a liquid, it **condenses**.

*Clouds and rain form when water vapor in the air **condenses** and forms droplets of water.*

Word Roots and Origins

Condense means "make dense." When something condenses, the molecules in it get closer together. It gets denser.

Related word: condensation

You can see **condensation** on the grass on some mornings. The grass is covered in small drops of water called dew.

conserve

When people decide not to use something, they **conserve** it. People can also **conserve** something by using less of it than they normally would. It is important to **conserve** things such as water, trees, and fuel so that they will last longer.

*You can help **conserve** water by taking shorter showers. You can **conserve** trees by using both sides of a sheet of paper. You can **conserve** oil and gas by walking instead of driving.*

> **Related word: conservation**
>
> *Water **conservation** is even more important when there is a drought.*

core

The center of a planet is its **core**.

*Earth's **core** is made mostly of iron.*

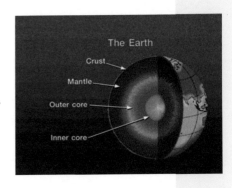

The Earth
Crust
Mantle
Outer core
Inner core

crust

The solid outer layer of a planet is the **crust**.

*The **crust** underneath the oceans is only about 5 kilometers thick. The **crust** that makes up the continents is about 40 kilometers thick.*

crystal

A **crystal** is a solid whose atoms are arranged in a repeating pattern. Some **crystals** are too small to see. Others are large, perfect geometric shapes.

*Quartz **crystals** have six sides and have a hexagonal shape.*

*Pyrite **crystals** have six sides, but are cube shaped.*

*All minerals form **crystals**.*

Related words: crystalline, crystallize

*Granite is a **crystalline** rock. It is made entirely of crystals.*

*Salt **crystallizes** from salt water. The crystals form after the water evaporates.*

---

current

A **current** is a steady flow of a liquid, a gas, or even a solid. There are **currents** of water in the oceans, **currents** of air in the atmosphere, and **currents** of rock deep inside the Earth.

*The Gulf Stream is an ocean **current**. Water in the Gulf Stream flows from the Gulf of Mexico north toward Europe.*

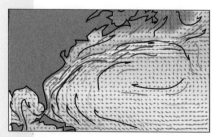

EARtH AND spAce scIeNce

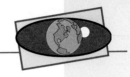

cycle

A **cycle** is something that happens over and over. In a **cycle**, things move from place to place. When something is in a **cycle**, it comes back to its original place. The water **cycle**, the carbon **cycle**, and the nutrient **cycle** are important to life on Earth.

*Evaporation and precipitation are both part of the water **cycle**.*

Word Roots and Origins

Cycle comes from the Greek word *kyklos*, which means "circle" or "wheel." To illustrate a cycle, you would draw a circle.

Related word: cyclic

Something that happens in a cycle is **cyclic**. The seasons are **cyclic**. We have spring then summer then fall then winter, and then spring again.

---

deposition

Deposition happens when rocks settle out of the air or water.

*The **deposition** of pebbles may form a beach.*

Related word: deposit

*The Mississippi River **deposits** mud on the ocean floor.*

earthquake

Earthquakes happen when large rocks break. This causes the ground to shake.

*In 1985 a strong **earthquake** damaged Mexico City.*

eclipse

When an object in space casts its shadow on another object, an **eclipse** takes place.

*When the Moon moves through Earth's shadow, a lunar **eclipse** takes place.*

*The Moon is right between the Earth and the Sun in this photograph of a solar **eclipse**.*

energy

Energy is anything that makes things happen. There are different forms of **energy**. These include solar **energy**, electricity, and nuclear **energy**.

*Energy from the Sun is called solar **energy**.*

Word Roots and Origins

The word *energy* comes from the Greek word *energeia*, which means "activity."

EARTH AND SPACE SCIENCE

environment

Everything that surrounds you is part of your **environment**. The **environment** includes plants, animals, rocks, water, air, and even buildings.

> **Related words: environmentalist, environmental**
>
> An **environmentalist** *cares about the health of the environment.*
>
> **Environmental** *issues include water quality and air pollution.*

erosion

Erosion happens when something such as water, wind, gravity, or ice breaks rocks apart and carries them away.

*Because of **erosion**, the Appalachian Mountains are not as tall as they used to be.*

> **Word Roots and Origins**
>
> The word *erode* comes from the Latin word *rodere*, which means "gnaw" or "eat away." The wind can gnaw holes in rock.
>
> **Related word: erode**
>
> *Rain and snow **erode** the Himalayas by about two millimeters every year.*

evaporate

When something **evaporates**, it turns from a liquid into a gas.

*After it rains, some of the water seeps into the ground, but some of it **evaporates**. It goes back into the air.*

> **Related word: evaporation**
>
> *After a lot of **evaporation**, lakes are not as deep as they used to be.*

fault

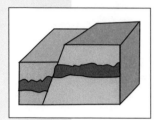

When large rocks break, they can move along a surface called a **fault**.

*Most earthquakes take place along **faults**.*

fertile

Soil that plants grow in easily is **fertile** soil.

*There are many farms near rivers because the soil there is so **fertile**. It is full of the minerals and other nutrients that plants need in order to grow.*

Related words: fertilize, fertilizer

*When farmers have trouble getting their crops to grow, they may decide to **fertilize** the fields. They put **fertilizer** on the fields to make the soil more fertile.*

---

fossil

A **fossil** is the evidence of a living thing that died thousands or millions of years ago. **Fossils** include bones, shells, and impressions, like footprints.

*Scientists study **fossils** to understand what life was like millions of years ago.*

Word Roots and Origins

The word *fossil* comes from the Latin word *fossilis*, which means "obtain by digging." Many fossils are found in rocks underground.

Related words: fossilize, fossilized, fossiliferous

It can take millions of years for a tree to **fossilize.**

The best place to find **fossilized** *leaves is inside mudstone or sandstone rock.*

Fossiliferous *limestone is full of fossils of sea animals.*

---

fossil fuel

Fossil fuels are made of plants and animals that lived millions of years ago. These fuels can be burned to make heat or electricity.

Coal is a **fossil fuel** *that is made of plants. Oil is a* **fossil fuel** *that is made of tiny sea organisms.*

galaxy

A **galaxy** is a group of millions of stars in space.

Our **galaxy** *is called the Milky Way* **galaxy.**

Word Roots and Origins

The word *galaxy* comes from the Greek word *gala*, which means "milk." If you look at our galaxy without using a telescope, it looks white like milk.

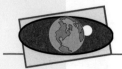

glacier

A **glacier** is a large river of ice that flows downhill very slowly.

*The **glacier** covering Greenland is made of ice that is more than two kilometers thick.*

Word Roots and Origins

The word *glacier* comes from the French word *glace*, which means "ice."

Related words: glaciation, glacial

*During the last **glaciation**, huge glaciers covered large parts of North America.*

*The Great Lakes are **glacial**. They were carved out by glaciers.*

---

greenhouse effect

The **greenhouse effect** happens when heat from the Sun is trapped inside a planet's atmosphere. On Earth the greenhouse effect is getting stronger, making Earth's climate change slowly.

*Because of the **greenhouse effect** on the planet Venus, the air there is hotter than 450°C.*

Word Roots and Origins

A greenhouse is a house with clear glass walls and a glass roof. It is used to grow plants. Sunlight travels through the glass and heats up the air inside the greenhouse. Then the warm air cannot escape.

Related words: greenhouse gas

Gases that cause the greenhouse effect are know as
greenhouse gases. They include water, carbon dioxide,
and methane.

groundwater

Groundwater is water that is in the rock
below Earth's surface.

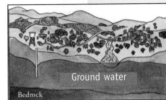

Ground water

Bedrock

*People drill wells in order to get **groundwater**.*

half-life

The atoms of some elements decay, or break down, to form
new atoms. The **half-life** is the time it takes for half of
all the atoms in the universe to decay.

*Uranium-238 has a **half-life** of about 4.5 billion years.
In 4.5 billion years, there will be only half as many
uranium-238 atoms in the universe as there are today.*

*Carbon-14 has a **half-life** of just 5,730 years. There were
twice as many carbon-14 atoms 5,730 years ago as there
are today.*

igneous rock

Igneous rock forms when hot liquid rock hardens. It can
form on the surface of a planet or deep underground.

*Granite and basalt are two kinds of **igneous rock**.*

Word Roots and Origins

Igneous comes from the Latin word *ignis*, which
means "fire."

lava

Lava is hot liquid rock on the surface of a planet.

*When Mauna Loa erupts, **lava** pours out of the volcano.*

Word Roots and Origins

The word *lava* probably comes from the Italian word *lava*, which means "fast-moving stream." In Italy, streams of lava come pouring down from the volcano Vesuvius.

lithosphere

The outermost part of the Earth is divided into about twelve pieces, called plates. These plates are made of a layer of hard rock called **lithosphere**. The **lithosphere** is made up of the Earth's crust and part of the Earth's mantle.

Word Roots and Origins

Lithos is the Greek word for "rock."

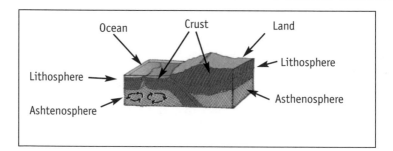

magma

Magma is liquid rock that is found underground.

*The mountains in Yosemite National Park are made of rock that formed when **magma** cooled slowly deep underground.*

EARTH AND SPACE SCIENCE

mantle

The layer between a planet's crust and a planet's core is called the **mantle**.

*Earth's **mantle** is made of solid rock. It is about 2,850 kilometers thick.*

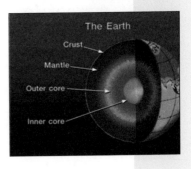

The Earth

Crust

Mantle

Outer core

Inner core

metamorphic rock

A **metamorphic rock** is a rock that has been changed by heat or pressure.

*Marble is a **metamorphic rock** that forms when limestone is buried and heated.*

Related word: metamorphose

*It takes millions of years for limestone to **metamorphose** and form marble.*

Word Roots and Origins

Meta means "change," and *morph* means "form." When a rock metamorphoses, new minerals can form in it and it can change shape.

---

meteor

A **meteor** is a rock from space that burns up as it falls through Earth's atmosphere. At night, it looks like a streak of light against the dark of the sky. Meteors are also known as "shooting stars."

*The Perseid **meteor** showers take place between July and August every year. During this event 80 to 200 **meteors** per hour shoot through the sky.*

meteorite

A **meteorite** is a rock that falls from space and lands on the surface of a planet.

*Nakhla is a famous **meteorite** that fell in Egypt. Scientists think that it originally came from the planet Mars. Most **meteorites** come from the asteroid belt, between Mars and Jupiter.*

Word Roots and Origins

The words *meteor* and *meteorite* come from the Greek word *meteoron*, which means "thing high up."

Related word: meteoroid

A **meteoroid** is a rock that is floating in space. If a **meteoroid** gets too close to Earth, it falls toward it. If it burns up, it becomes a meteor. If it hits the ground, it becomes a meteorite.

---

mineral

Most rocks are made of **minerals**. A **mineral** is a substance that forms naturally and that has a specific chemical composition. All **minerals** form crystals.

*Quartz, topaz, and diamond are examples of **minerals**.*

moon

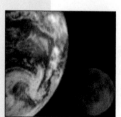

A **moon** is the natural satellite of a planet. **Moons** orbit their planets. That is, they travel around their planets.

*The **Moon** is Earth's **moon**. Jupiter has more than sixty **moons**. The largest are Ganymede, Callisto, Io, and Europa.*

nonrenewable

A resource is **nonrenewable** if it cannot be replaced easily after it is used up.

*Oil and gas are **nonrenewable** resources. Once we have burned all the oil we take from the ground, there will be none left.*

orbit

An **orbit** is the path an object in space takes when it travels around another object.

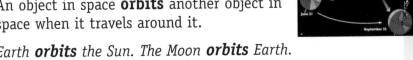

*The **orbit** of the Moon is nearly a circle.*
An object in space **orbits** another object in space when it travels around it.

*Earth **orbits** the Sun. The Moon **orbits** Earth.*

ore

An **ore** is a mineral or rock that has one or more useful metals in it.

*Bauxite is an aluminum **ore**. Most aluminum that people use comes from bauxite.*

*Hematite is an iron **ore** mineral. Iron **ore** is used to make steel.*

planet

A **planet** is a large ball of rock or gas that orbits a star.

*There are nine **planets** that orbit the Sun: Mercury, Venus, Earth, Mars, Jupiter, Saturn, Uranus, Neptune, and Pluto.*

Word Roots and Origins

The word *planet* comes from the Greek word for "wanderer." If you watch a planet, it appears to wander across the sky while the stars seem to stay in one place.

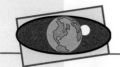
plate

The Earth's surface is made of about a dozen large pieces called **plates**. These **plates** fit together like pieces of a puzzle. **Plates** are made of lithosphere (crust and part of the mantle).

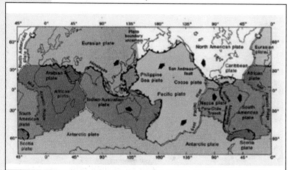

*The South American **plate** and the African **plate** are slowly moving away from each other.*

Related words: plate tectonics

Earth's plates move. In some places they crash into each other. In some places they move away from each other. In some places they grind past each other. The movements shape Earth's surface.

This is called **plate tectonics.**

---

poles

Earth has two kinds of **poles**: geographic **poles** and magnetic **poles**.

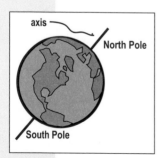

The geographic **poles** are the places where Earth's axis and Earth's surface intersect. There are two geographic **poles**: north and south. The North **Pole** is located in the Arctic Ocean. The South **Pole** is in Antarctica.

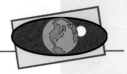

*The North **Pole** is always covered in ice.*

*Roald Amundsen was the first explorer to reach the South **Pole**.*

The magnetic **poles** are the places on Earth where the ends of a magnet point to. There are two magnetic **poles**: magnetic north and magnetic south. Compass needles point to magnetic north.

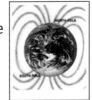

*Earth's magnetic **poles** move around very slowly over time. Once in a while, they switch places. Then north becomes south and south becomes north.*

pollution

Pollution is the act of poisoning the air, water, and land. There are different kinds of **pollution**.

*There is a lot of **pollution** of the air in large cities.*

> **Related words: pollute, pollutant**
>
> *Factories must pay a fine if they **pollute** too much.*
>
> *It is important not to put **pollutants** into the air or water.*

renewable

A resource is **renewable** if it cannot be used up or if it can be replaced easily. Water, wind, sunlight, soil, and trees are all **renewable**. If you cut down a tree and use it to make paper, you can grow a new tree to replace it.

*It is important to conserve water resources, even though they are **renewable.***

resource

A natural **resource** is something that people use that comes from the Earth. Air, water, plants, animals, soil, rocks, and minerals are all **resources**.

*Plant **resources** are used for food, clothing, and medicine.*

satellite

A **satellite** is an object that travels around a larger object in space. Some **satellites** are artificial. That is, they are made by people. Others are natural. A natural **satellite** is also called a moon.

*Galileo discovered Jupiter's four largest **satellites**: Ganymede, Callisto, Io, and Europa. There are hundreds of artificial **satellites** orbiting Earth.*

They are used for science and communication.

Word Roots and Origins

Satellite comes from the Latin word that means "follower." Satellites orbit planets while planets orbit stars. Our satellites follow the Earth around the Sun.

sediment

Sediment is material that is taken from one place to another place by wind, water, ice, or even gravity. **Sediment** is made of broken pieces of rocks, shells, and plant and animal remains. Sand and mud are two examples of **sediments**.

*When the river flooded, it left a layer of **sediment** in the fields.*

Word Roots and Origins

The word *sediment* comes from the Latin word *sedere*, which means "sink" or "settle down." Sediments settle out of the air and water.

sedimentary rock

When layers of sediment are pressed together over a long period of time, they become a hard rock called **sedimentary rock**. Sandstone, for example, is a **sedimentary rock** made of sand.

The Washington Monument is made of a **sedimentary rock** *called limestone.*

smog

Smog is a type of air pollution. **Smog** forms when sunlight interacts with pollution given off by cars and factories. It makes the air look gray, yellow, or orange.

In December 1952, the **smog** *in London was so thick that people could not see well enough to drive. Hundreds of people died because the air was so poisonous.*

Word Roots and Origins

The word *smog* is a mixture of two other words: *smoke* and *fog*.

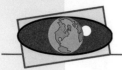

solar system

A **solar system** is a star and all the objects that orbit it. Our **solar system** is made of the Sun, the nine planets, the asteroids, the comets, and all the dust and gas in between.

*Astronomers think that the **Solar System** is about 4.6 billion years old.*

> ### Word Roots and Origins
> *Solar* comes from the word *sol*, which means "sun."

star

A **star** is a large ball of hot, glowing gas.

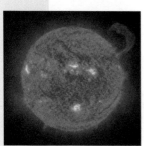

*The closest **star** to Earth is the Sun.*

*There are billions of **stars** in the universe, but without a telescope, you cannot see more than a thousand.*

> ### Related word: stellar
> Anything related to stars is **stellar**.
>
> *Jane studies **stellar** evolution. She wants to know how stars change over time.*

uplift

Uplift happens when large rock formations rise up. **Uplift** forms mountains.

*The Rocky Mountains in Colorado began to be **uplifted** about 70 million years ago.*

volcano

A **volcano** is an opening on a planet's surface where lava flows out. A **volcano** can also be a hill or a mountain made of cooled, hardened lava.

*Mauna Loa in Hawaii is the largest **volcano** on Earth.*

*Olympus Mons, on Mars, is the biggest **volcano** in the Solar System.*

Related words: volcanic

Volcanic rocks form when lava turns solid.

Basalt is a **volcanic** rock.

Word Roots and Origins

Vulcan was the Greek god of fire. He was a blacksmith (someone who makes objects out of iron) whose workshops were inside volcanoes.

waste

Waste is anything made by people that they can't use. Trash is **waste**. Hazardous **waste** is **waste** that is poisonous or dangerous.

*People haven't decided how to get rid of nuclear **waste**.*

water cycle

Heat from the Sun evaporates water from the surface of the land, rivers, lakes, and oceans. Water vapor rises into the air and forms clouds. When the water vapor condenses into liquid, it falls back down as rain. The rain enters the soil, rivers, lakes, and oceans. The **water cycle** continues.

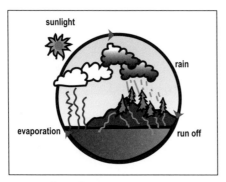

weathering

Weathering is the breakdown of rocks and minerals by air and water.

Weathering causes the iron in rock to turn to rust.

Related words: weather, weathered

*When iron **weathers,** it forms rust.*

*Limestone statues can get so **weathered** that it is impossible to read the words carved into them.*

EARth AND spAce scieNce

Notes:

INDeX

A

abiotic 7
accelerate 36
acid rain 68
adaptation 7
alloy 36
antibiotic 7
aquifer 68
asteroid 68
asthenosphere 69
atmosphere 69
atom 37
axis 70

B

bacteria 8
behavior 8
biodiversity 9
biosphere 9
biosphere 70
biotic 9
boil 37

C

camouflage 10
carbon 10
carbon 38
carbon cycle 70
cell 11
chemical 38
chemical bond 38
chemical change 39

chlorophyll 11
chromosome 12
circuit, electric 40
classification 12
climate 71
combustion 12
combustion 40
combustion 71
comet 72
community 13
compound 41
condense 41
condense 72
conductor, electrical 41
conductor, heat 42
conserve 13
conserve 73
constant 1
consumer 14
convection 42
core 73
crest, wave 42
crust 73
crystal 43
crystal 74
current 74
current, electric 43
cycle 75

INDex